4751

DRUGS DRINKS & MORALS

DRUGS DRINKS & MORALS

by
Mark E. Petersen

Published by Deseret Book Company 1969

Library of Congress No. 79-109605.

Copyright © 1969
by
Deseret Book Company

LITHOGRAPHED BY

IN THE UNITED STATES OF AMERICA

Contents

A Plunge to Death ----------------------------- 1
Art's Appeal ------------------------------ 5
The "Dope" on Drugs ---------------------- 10
The Cost of Thrills ------------------------- 17
Liquor Is Also Involved -------------------- 21
Not Everyone Drinks! ---------------------- 25
Liquor: Ally of Crime --------------------- 29
Tobacco Is Also Blamed -------------------- 36
Morals Are Involved ---------------------- 41
The Wages of Sin ------------------------- 45
Ever Hear of Chastity? -------------------- 52
Dress and Morality ------------------------ 57
Protective Commandments ------------------ 62
Avoid Pornography ----------------------- 66
We Have a Destiny! ---------------------- 71

"Repent, and turn yourselves from all your transgressions; so iniquity shall not be your ruin.

"Cast away from you all your transgressions, whereby ye have transgressed; and make you a new heart and a new spirit: for why will ye die, O house of Israel?

"For I have no pleasure in the death of him that dieth, saith the Lord God: wherefore turn yourselves, and live ye."
(Ezekiel 18:30-32)

Diane Linkletter as she appeared when playing at the Valley Music Hall in Salt Lake City.

Chapter One

A Plunge to Death

"It was murder," sobbed grieving Art Linkletter as he gazed down at the broken body of his twenty-year-old daughter Diane.

"It was suicide," said the police who investigated Diane's plunge from a sixth-story window.

Who was right? Or were both right?

Newspaper reports described it this way:

Diane had joined an "in" crowd in Hollywood. But to be "in" meant indulgence with the rest of the "in" crowd, and that included using drugs. So Diane took up the habit. Not that she enjoyed it, because she didn't, but being "in" was all-important to her.

She was beautiful and she was popular. She also was inclined to be emotional.

Drugs were not good for her, and she knew it. Her parents did too, and tried to persuade her to stop using them. But are they good for anyone?

Diane tried to tell herself that what she was taking was harmless and only gave her a lift. This is the old song they all sing. But it was different from a lift—it was a trip—out of reality—and into a whole new psychological world, she would say.

Then she started using LSD. It really did things to her—changed her life—brought new experiences—made a tremendous change in her mind and in her personality, her outlook and her desires. But all for the worse.

And then, sitting with her boy friend one day, and under the influence of LSD, she suddenly went into one of those fantastic emotional eruptions so common to drug addicts, especially to users of LSD.

Obviously driven out of her mind by the drug, and talking and screaming insanely, she dashed to an open window and plunged six stories to her death.

This was her trip, but it was not the trip out of reality that she had hoped for when she took the drug. The ground to which she fell was very real indeed, and very hard. It made no allowance for her emotions nor for her drug-induced lack of mental control. It showed no mercy, and had no way of softening the fall.

The ambulance was real too, and so were the men who wrapped her in a blanket, bleeding from head and body, and took her away.

Her trip—now so very real—included a stop at the mortuary where she was laid on a slab, not an imaginary one, but one made of marble. Other unfortunates had been stretched out on that slab before her, and had

A Plunge to Death

gone the only way now open to her: to a very real cold and silent grave.

It was a new kind of "in" for Diane. But it was the inevitable one for her and for all others who take "trips" into the unreal, only to learn that nothing about life is unreal. Reality is life itself, and life is a stern reality.

But now, for Diane, which was it, murder or suicide?

Diane's death stirred Art Linkletter as nothing else had ever done. And most important of all, his great soul was moved to help others afflicted as was his lovely daughter.

He said that the people who sold her that drug were responsible for her death. That is why he called it murder. "They killed her," he said, those vicious ones who traffic in death for money, money literally squeezed out of the life blood of the addicts who will do anything to get another trip.

Linkletter determined that Diane's death must not be in vain. Now it must serve a mighty purpose in the lives of other young people. It could save them from a similar fate if only they would listen—listen to the facts—listen to reality, and profit by it!

As the noted entertainer pondered over the tragic conclusion to his daughter's promising career, he appealed to parents everywhere to join the fight against drugs, and he pleaded with all young people to avoid their use.

Parents as well as younger people should learn the

truth about drugs, he tearfully said as he planned the burial services for Diane; and about alcohol and other narcotics also, and "get the information in a rememberable, sensible, non-panic way—repetitively."

Chapter Two

Art's Appeal

In private graveside services at Forest Lawn Memorial Park, the Linkletter family buried Diane, whose death they blame on LSD—"a tiger in her bloodstream," the Associated Press reported.

From the fifth grade up, the entertainer said, children "should be grounded as thoroughly in the dangers of putting chemicals into their systems as they are in walking across a superhighway with their eyes shut."

The television star and businessman, already a lecturer to college and other groups on "the permissiveness of this society," said:

"I intend now to step that up and give it much more point. I think my daughter's death is going to be paid for many, many times by the kinds of things I can say and get done, using this as an example.

"Since this has happened to Diane, you cannot imagine the number of people who have called, wired, written me—important people, well known, who have daughters in sanitariums, sons in sanitariums, children who have killed themselves. They have hushed this up as a terrible family secret.

"All of a sudden they're coming out and telling me" . . . his voice choked and halted . . . "They'll join me—" in publicizing these evils?

"Yes," he said. "Many are lawyers, bankers, so-called community pillars of decency . . . journalists." He knows none personally.

Linkletter, 57, told the Associated Press he doesn't have all the answers, but "I've been as good a parent as I could possibly be, I think. We've been a very close family. We've done everything you do according to the book—taken vacations together, gone on pack trips together, traveled extensively all over the world.

"We've been a good Christian family. My wife and I have tried to set a good example by being a good example.

"We have tried to keep our children up to date on what the dangerous things are, but perhaps we did not bear down as hard as we should have.

"Diane, of all the children, was always the most daring. She was the most emotionally up and down. She was either on top of the mountain or in the valley of despair—over trivial things.

"She was the one who would dare to sneak out at

night, and be willing to accept the punishment for it. If she came in later than she was supposed to come in, as she did frequently, she got a tongue lashing and took it in good spirits.

"Of course, becoming an actress, as she was training to be, was absolutely perfect for her because she had the emotional heights and emotional lows that could have done a lot for her as a career actress. She would charm the birds right out of the trees.

"So when I heard, indirectly, that she might be going with a group that was experimenting around, I brought it out, as I do everything.

"Our lines of communication were open as far as I was concerned. I said, 'Is it true, Diane, that this group has been experimenting with some of the new things?' And she admitted that it was true.

"I pointed out to her the obvious dangers. She agreed and with consummate skill acted out the part that she would never do it again. Obviously she did it again.

"Her mother would have talks with her, good long talks about what was going on among the children of today. My daughter would tell Lois what some of the other girls were doing and how worried she was.

"We now know that she probably was voicing worries about herself, worries that began to gnaw at her. SHE WAS CONCERNED THAT SHE HAD QUIT AND WAS STILL HAVING RECURRING HIGHS

SHE COULDN'T CONTROL. (It had been many weeks since she had taken the drug, but its effects persisted.)

"OVER THE MONTHS SHE FOUND SHE HAD A TIGER IN HER BLOODSTREAM.

"Apparently what finally happened was she was despondent over a spat with her boy friend and took a much stronger dose of this poison. SHE WAS WORRIED THAT SHE WOULD NEVER COME OUT OF IT MENTALLY, AND THIS LED TO HER DEATH.

"Parents can feel they have all the lines of communication open. But you can't live with your children all the time. They've got to be by themselves. It's impossible to create an atmosphere in which there can be no contamination."

So what can parents do? Get information on drugs from the Department of Health, Education and Welfare, or any city or state health department, Linkletter said, and get it to their children along with—

"Such things as dinnertime reading of newspaper stories that will confirm this, which is one of the reasons I gave this story to the papers.

"I WANT THE PARENTS, AND I WANT THEIR KIDS, TO READ ABOUT THIS AND BE SHOCKED, BE FRIGHTENED AT WHAT CAN HAPPEN.

"What you have to do is not just say using drugs is a bad thing but have incontestable scientific proof. And when somebody like Timothy Leary comes out and justifies it, we have got to jump on him with hobnailed boots. Such people are casting doubt on the authority of people who know how deadly these things can be."

Chapter Three

The "Dope" on Drugs

Shakespeare wrote about "a rose by any other name." He knew that names are important, but not conclusive in identification.

People talk today about things that "turn you on." It may be an exciting type of music, or certain kinds of companionship, or even substances that take you on a "trip." Speaking in today's parlance they all "turn you on."

The immediate question that arises is: Turn you on to what?

Companionships can "turn you on," it is true, into either safe paths or dangerous ones, into a good life or its opposite. They become junction points having both right turns and wrong ones. It is admitted that they "turn you on," always toward your next step in life. But what kind of a step will it be?

The "Dope" on Drugs

One of today's greatest "turner oners," as the youngsters put it, is the use of drugs. And what do they do, help you or hurt you?

They can send you insane! This they have done to thousands of young Americans.

In one state mental hospital admissions of individuals for emotional problems resulting from the use of drugs have gone up in a ratio of one to 47 in a two-year period. Another large hospital reports that within a year there has been an increase of 400 percent in the number of youngsters aged 18 to 20 admitted with serious mental problems resulting from the use of drugs.

Presumptions on the part of some young people—sometimes encouraged by certain ones who claim some medical knowledge—that marijuana is no more harmful than tobacco, are proving to be completely false.

Marijuana, like tobacco, is habit-forming, but it is also destructive of mental health, and can destroy the entire future of young people who indulge.

The more powerful drugs, beyond any question, are causing mental problems of such seriousness that some of the patients may never recover.

In one typical community, as reported by the Associated Press recently, where 3,000 babies are born annually, one child in every five will require mental health service because of the stimulants taken by the mothers, and at least 240 of those 3,000 will become patients in mental hospitals. All because their mothers wanted something to "turn them on."

Is this the kind of "turning on" that Latter-day Saints want?

The entire Associated Press dispatch, dated out of Washington, D.C., reads:

"U.S. government health officials have pictured the United States as beset with burgeoning problems of alcoholism, mental illness, venereal disease and drug use.

"On top of that, the officials said, health-care costs are skyrocketing.

"In testimony before a House subcommittee they reported:

"There are up to 6.5 million alcoholics in the land, and their number grows by 200,000 annually. A growing percentage are married, middle-aged women of the middle and upper classes.

"IN A TYPICAL COMMUNITY OF 150,000 POPULATION, WHERE 3,000 CHILDREN ARE BORN ANNUALLY, ONE OF FIVE WILL REQUIRE SOME FORM OF MENTAL-HEALTH SERVICE AND 240 WILL BE PATIENTS IN MENTAL HOSPITALS IN THEIR LIFETIME.

"GONORRHEA IS OUT OF CONTROL WITH A 12 PERCENT INCREASE IN REPORTED CASES IN EACH OF THE LAST FEW YEARS. IN SOME POPULATION GROUPS ONE OF THREE HAVE THIS VENEREAL DISEASE AND DON'T KNOW IT.

"All economic groups and all age groups are involved in taking the mind-expanding drug LSD, but it is falling off in colleges and high schools because of the publicity about its dangers.

The "Dope" on Drugs

"The testimony before a House Appropriations subcommittee came from Dr. William Stewart, U.S. Surgeon General; Dr. Stanley F. Yolles, director of the National Institute of Mental Health, and Dr. David J. Spencer, director of the National Communicable Disease Center."

What makes teenagers such easy prey to the drug craze?

Dr. Victor H. Vogel, chief medical officer of the U.S. government hospital for control of drugs, at Lexington, Kentucky, says:

"They are just pleasure-seeking kids who were following the fashion of the school or the community and tragically found that after using drugs they had a wildcat by the tail and couldn't let go. When asked if they would have still experimented with drugs if they had known they would get 'hooked,' they said, 'Of course not.'"

And as Dr. Robert V. Seliger, noted fellow of the American Psychiatric Association, expressed it, "They didn't know the gun was loaded."

Dr. Seliger then asks:

"How does a youngster become an addict? Alcoholism and drug addiction have this in common: both begin with the desire for a cheap thrill, a desire to be one of the crowd. Most alcoholics began as social drinkers. Most youthful drug addicts started with innocent-appearing marijuana.

"Actually, marijuana is as dangerous as a pile of

greasy old rags left in the bottom of a closet. The first 'drag' on a 'reefer' throws in the first greasy rag that leads to the combustion of heroin. It is because the youngster thinks he can 'get away with it.' He wants a 'bigger boot,' thus making himself fair game for the heroin 'pusher.'

"Perhaps the 'pusher' was once a thrill-seeking kid like himself who is now an addict and supports his expensive habit by selling dope. An infectious habit addiction INVARIABLY BEGINS WITH ASSOCIATION WITH ANOTHER ADDICT. These 'Typhoid Marys' are only too glad to pass out FREE SAMPLES at first, and to jeer down any show of reluctance by taunts of 'chicken' and 'square.' By the same false reasoning, a youngster might as well be called 'chicken' if he refused to hold a lighted stick of dynamite or a 'square' if he could not be dared into jumping out a 30th floor window. If a youngster has only elementary horse sense, he will not be a victim in the first place," said Dr. Seliger.

When a person first begins to use marijuana, it produces an irritating effect on the bronchial mucous membranes and will likely cause severe coughing, accompanied by a heavy flow of saliva.

With some it may induce feelings of exultation and increased strength with a distinct drop in control of the emotions. The smoker may begin to boast, dance, shout or otherwise act out of control.

During this stage, which may last for from one to four hours, according to Dr. Seliger, opposition or attempted restraint on the part of others may excite a frenzy in the smoker, leading him to almost any kind of violence. It is well known, the learned doctor explains, that many criminals often "prime" themselves for desperate acts by smoking this vicious weed.

The second stage in using marijuana may with some people take the form of illusions of sight and hearing. Dr. Seliger said that in this condition, because their sensory systems are highly stimulated, they may describe beautiful things they imagine they are seeing or hearing, so far out of their minds are they.

But Dr. Seliger explains that all of this is then followed by a period of deep depression which may result in loss of balance, staggering, and numbness ending in a long sleep. Smoking marijuana definitely prevents proper perception and distorts time, distance, and sound. Continued use usually will bloat the face, make the legs tremulous and weak, and cause both mental and moral degeneration.

Then the learned doctor says:

"If there were any scientific, medical use for marijuana, physicians would hesitate to prescribe it because of its potentially vicious result.

"Now, let us take a brief look at heroin, a present-day terror of American youth. This drug is five times more potent than morphine. As we have previously indicated, heroin carries with it so much danger of addiction that physicians no longer prescribe it and its manufacture or sale in the United States is forbidden by law.

"This dangerous, enslaving drug (heroin) produces a severe physical craving for more of it and at the same time makes its user a destroyer, a killer, a committer of almost any crime.

"Heroin is so terrible in its effects that physicians have hesitated even to talk about it or to write about it, yet suddenly (especially in some large cities) it becomes easy for young people to purchase it in many neighborhoods, especially near schools. Let us again quote Dr. Victor H. Vogel, formerly Medical Officer in Charge of the United States Public Health Service Hospital at Lexington, Kentucky:

"'Without exception, the teenage addicts first smoked marijuana more or less intermittently for a period before becoming curious as to the effects of sniffing heroin, which suddenly became highly recommended for pleasure use.'

"Since marijuana and heroin are with us despite all of our laws forbidding the sale or use of either, the time seems to have come when physicians and others must at least mention dangerous and illegal narcotics if they are to be successful in asking young people to use common sense when a 'friend' suggests to them or 'dares' them to 'take' a few puffs on a 'reefer.' Sound information, good home training, and this plain common sense can do more than all laws to prevent the spread of youthful addiction."

Chapter Four

The Cost of Thrills

Dr. Robert V. Seliger, of the American Psychiatric Association, writing for "School and College Service," Columbus, Ohio, warns teenagers without reservation against the use of drugs. He says:

"A teenager doesn't always use common sense. He may just want thrills. And, after the first vomiting attack, sniffing heroin gives him a 'big bang.'

"But it doesn't last long and he shifts to injections. The trouble is that he must have more and bigger 'shots' to give him anything like the pleasure he felt at first.

"Then he suddenly finds that instead of having fun, he merely becomes groggy from heroin and must continue to take it if he is to live with any degree of comfort at all.

"For, without his four to six or more shots a day,

he suffers horribly in every nerve and muscle in his body. Now he will do anything to get dope.

"EVERY MAN, WOMAN, AND CHILD SHOULD KNOW THAT HEROIN ADDICTION OFTEN BEGINS WITH MARIJUANA AND THAT THE USE OF HEROIN IS A HABIT THAT CANNOT VOLUNTARILY BE STOPPED.

"They should also know that it is similarly difficult to stop the habit of using other narcotics that may be smuggled into this country as contraband or that may be legally available but forbidden to be sold without a prescription.

"Since it costs him at least $10.00 a day for heroin, a boy may turn to stealing from his family, then to more serious theft. A girl may resort to prostitution or shoplifting.

"The sooner they come to the attention of the juvenile authorities, the more fortunate they are, because their best chance for survival depends upon prompt treatment at a hospital like one of our government hospitals, located at Lexington, Kentucky, and Fort Worth, Texas.

"The minimum length of treatment required at either of these hospitals is four and a half months. Unfortunately, overcrowding makes the situation difficult for teenagers.

"They are of necessity thrown into contact with other addicts whose lifetime history of treatment and relapses offers them scant encouragement. Aside from this, however, the outlook for youngsters is hopeful."

Dr. Seliger then flatly asks the youth of today:

"WHAT KIND OF THRILLS DO YOU WANT? Life, which is beginning for you, has many fine thrills in store—the thrill of achievement, the thrill of making friends you admire, the thrill of love, marriage, parenthood, and the thrill or infinite satisfaction of winning the respect of yourself and of others.

"These are thrills that uplift and inspire you, and make of you a source of inspiration.

"COULD YOU POSSIBLY WANT THE SHORT TERM THRILL OF DRUG ADDICTION—ADDICTION THAT TAKES FROM YOU AT THE VERY LEAST YOUR REPUTATION AND COULD LIKELY MEAN HORRIBLE SUFFERING, DEGRADATION, AND DEATH?"

As young Latter-day Saints, what is the principal objective of our lives? Is it a noble aim to drug one's self into a stupor, thus becoming irresponsible, weak, a prey to every predatory person?

Is a "trip" taken mentally by the use of a drug so desirable that one would risk his sanity for the rest of his life to "enjoy" it? Is there anything desirable in hallucination anyway? Or is it the clear cool mind that assures success and true and permanent happiness?

And what can give us this clarity of mind?

Clean living. Good health. Spirituality, and freedom from stimulants of all kinds, including alcohol.

Inspiration from heaven is available to every one of us under proper conditions. The constant guidance of the

Holy Spirit is promised to us if we live as we know we should.

Which is to be preferred—divine inspiration or hallucinations?

Which encourages success in school or at work—inspiration or a drug-induced stupor?

Which will help to preserve chastity—divine guidance or addiction to demoralizing narcotics?

Which will give us proper standing in the world—a clear mind or a clouded one?

So what is it that really "turns us on"? Only one thing: The Spirit of God, which comes to all who sincerely live the Gospel, and every faithful believer in Christ is entitled to its ministrations.

Chapter Five

Liquor Is Also Involved

It is a fact that most drug users also drink alcoholic beverages.

And it is also a fact that alcohol is now becoming one of the great menaces facing our modern way of life. What will you do about it?

Writing in "Seventeen" magazine, David Klein raised some pertinent questions on drinking.

Said he:

"When somebody puts a highball glass or a beer can in your hand or beckons you to the clubroom bar, it's a bit late in the game for you to start thinking about whether, what, or how much you plan to drink.

"This kind of decision you need to make ahead of time—and in an adult way—not by following what your crowd does, but by taking a hard look at the facts and weighing them carefully in terms of who and what you are."

This advice is something that every Latter-day Saint youth should heed. Mr. Klein makes it clear that this decision should not be made on a basis of "being a good sport," or rebelling against your parents or your religious principles.

He mentions that some people drink because "it makes me feel more at ease at a party." Latter-day Saints, of course, shouldn't go to parties where liquor is served. But if there are difficult circumstances requiring attendance at some "cocktail" function, certainly the Latter-day Saint will take soft drinks, and be proud of his standards.

And someone else says, "Everybody does it." This, of course, is not true, for at least 30 percent of the nation are complete abstainers, and another 30 percent drink so little that their liquor bill would not exceed five dollars in a year, according to official figures.

And someone else says he does not want to be a "wet blanket." That is weakness indeed. Again, good Latter-day Saints do not lower their standards for any such inane reason. And neither should they fraternize with people who would regard them as wet blankets because they have character and good habits.

Important people in this world know and respect the standards of the Mormon people, and they *expect* members of the Church to uphold them, and are disappointed if they do not do so.

President Heber J. Grant was intimately acquainted with a banker in New York who refused to hire a

Liquor Is Also Involved

Mormon for an important position because this church member smoked cigars with the banker.

"But you smoke," said the young man to the banker.

"Yes," said the banker, "but it is not against my religion. If you do not have the character to live your religion, you do not have the strength of character to work for this bank."

A Latter-day Saint newspaper publisher attended a convention of southern publishers. A cocktail period preceded the dinner. The Mormon was not aware that such a period was planned, and he walked directly into the ante-room of the dining hall and there found himself in the midst of a drinking group.

"This way," said the southern publisher who was host. "I know you do not drink, so I have tomato juice here waiting for you."

His remark was heard by all in the group. Everyone understood, and everyone expected the Mormon publisher to live up to his religion. It was not a part of their own creeds to avoid alcohol themselves, but they knew it was against the religion of the Latter-day Saints and would have been disappointed if their Mormon friend had not lived up to his standards.

Someone else has said, "My date expects me to take a drink." And what is the answer to that? Simply that we should not date with drinkers nor with people who expect us to drink.

If your date expects you to take a drink, he will expect even more afterward, when the alcohol has clouded your mind, eased your conscience, and lowered your protective bars.

Whenever your date expects you to drink, ask yourself why. He knows what alcohol will do to you, and he knows that when your resistance is low, anything might happen, and that is what some of the boys expect. One of our poets has said, "Vice is a monster of such dreadful mein that to be hated needs but to be seen. But seen too oft, familiar with her face, first we pity, then endure, and then embrace."

A study was recently made among high school students of Utah, Kansas, New York and Michigan. Among 8,000 high school boys questioned, fewer than half of them had as much as a glass of beer in a week. Very few of these "drinkers" said they would refuse to date a girl who does not drink. The study also showed that most non-drinking teenagers of both sexes are convinced that their schoolmates who do drink do so "to act smart."

For the Latter-day Saint, the path of safety is in upholding our standards. There can be no compromise with sin. And liquor leads to all manner of sin.

Chapter Six

Not Everyone Drinks!

Forty percent of the population of the United States admits fairly heavy drinking. Of course, among them are millions of alcoholics. But it is refreshing to know that 60 percent of the population drinks very little. Thirty percent of the nation is listed as complete abstainers. The other half of that 60 percent spend less than $5.00 per year on liquor, and at present prices, that amounts almost to abstinence.

Federal figures show that of the 117,000,000 adults in America, 5.9 percent drink nearly half of all the hard liquor consumed in this country. That is, they drink 47.8 percent of all the hard liquor that is drunk here.

It is interesting to note too that many men spend from $2.90 to $7.00 per day for liquor. It is a very expensive habit, financially, as well as in many other ways.

Statistics indicate that most teenagers who drink

learn to do so in their own homes, and that drinking parents not only set them the example, but actually provide the liquor for them.

This trend is creating consternation among the organizations now fighting alcoholism, who see in it a rapidly growing threat to the younger generation who are turning more and more to think mistakenly that liquor is the door to social acceptance.

But the fact that 60 percent of the population is virtually free from the use of liquor is most encouraging.

As many are now turning away from the use of tobacco for health reasons, so a good many are beginning to turn from liquor for the same reasons.

However, the liquor interests are invading certain groups heretofore thought to be fairly safe from their allurements.

At a recent convocation of Methodists, a relaxing of the church tenets against the use of alcohol was attempted, but was battled vigorously by those who sought to hold the line which had made Methodists famous in their fight against drink.

A survey had shown that 61 percent of Methodists above 15 years of age have used liquor at some time. Advocates of relaxing the stand of that church against its use argued that "the policy of abstinence is producing hypocrisy and a loss of integrity in the corporate life of the church and in the lives of many ministers and laymen."

It had been recommended that the church do away

with a pledge long held sacred among Methodists requiring clergymen to be complete abstainers, and that whether a layman drinks or not be left to the discretion of the individual.

These recommendations were fought vigorously and vehemently.

So far as Latter-day Saints are concerned, they can take but one position. If they believe in the revelations of the Lord to the Prophet Joseph Smith, they must be abstainers.

To make liquor more readily available is to add to the number of alcoholics. Who can tell which of us will become an alcoholic? Whose home will be wrecked? Whose virtue will be lost?

The liquor question is a moral one. Liquor at no time has added to virtue, stability or good character. Always it has had the opposite effect.

This is not to say that everyone who uses it is of weak character, for that would be an unjust statement.

But it is true that liquor is an evil which is weakening the nation as a whole, adding to the crime rate, leading many into acts which they would never commit if they were sober, and which constantly tends to break down home life and family ties.

Many people of the world do not regard the liquor evil as a moral problem. Particularly is this true of those who are known as "social drinkers."

Their churches do not teach them that there are divine laws against liquor, and they feel that social drinking is but a part of the normal way of life, as it may be for them.

But such cannot be the case with Latter-day Saints. The Lord commands us to avoid liquor. He does not say avoid the use of a lot of it, nor does he say that a little will do no harm. Not the Lord!

He tells us frankly and bluntly that alcoholic drinks are not good and therefore are not to be used at all. Latter-day Saints should be willing to obey him. They must admit that since the glory of God is intelligence, the great Creator is surely intelligent enough to know what is good and what is bad for us, since he made all things.

For us there can be only one position—avoid liquor and its demoralizing effects, even as we would any other evil.

Chapter Seven

Liquor: Ally of Crime

When 56 percent of a large group of criminals are heavy drinkers, what does it mean?

The British Association for the Advancement of Science is asking itself this question, and it is providing an answer as well: Liquor and crime are partners.

But not only are 56 percent of the prisoners in Britain heavy drinkers—virtually all other prisoners drink to some extent, and it is determined that liquor is a part of the kind of life a criminal lives when he is out of jail.

Two sociologists assigned to make the above-mentioned study were so convinced that liquor abets crime and lowers human beings into degradation that they made a detailed report on their findings at a convention of the scientific body.

They urged a still further study—more extensive

than their own—to further establish the facts about the relationship between liquor and crime.

Speaking of the prisoners they studied, these sociologists said:

"These people are often pathetic. Some have sunk right down to an existence of degradation beyond description. Some have been given help by a society similar to Alcoholics Anonymous time after time but still they go back to drink and destitution.

"Some of them seem beyond help and hope. The problem thus is one of prevention as well as treatment.

"No doubt a good deal of the blame, if blame it is, lies in the psychology and physiology of the victim," the sociologists went on, "but there are some individuals who seem equally to be the casualties of an inadequate society."

The comments of these sociologists are as applicable to America as they are to England. They should be studied and considered by every right-thinking person.

Note their main points:

1. Through liquor human beings can and do sink down to an existence of degradation beyond description, and many of them return to their drink time after time regardless of treatment.

2. That so far as liquor is concerned we have "an inadequate society."

It is sad enough to speak of the human derelicts who become almost "subhuman" through the degradation brought upon them by drink. But we must remember also the much more prevalent but less heralded results of drink in the lives of families afflicted by conflicts in the home—divorce, cruelty of parents to children, cruelty of parents to each other, squandering of needed money on drink which brings this degradation; absenteeism from jobs, inefficiency on the job, examples leading to juvenile delinquency, children being taught to drink in the home by errant parents, and numerous other problems.

No one yet has been able to measure the costs of liquor to the general public. It certainly cannot be counted in the money spent on its purchase, nor even in economics at all. When we think of the worth of a single human soul, and multiply it by the millions whose lives are adversely affected by liquor, it becomes almost beyond human comprehension.

And yet we still put up with it. That is where the "inadequate society" enters the problem.

When will society wake up to the real seriousness of this situation? Will closing our eyes to it solve it? Can giving in to selfish desires for so-called social drinking justify the risk of creating all this human destruction which is forever in the wake of a drinking society?

A single drink exposes any person to the full impact of alcoholism. Who knows when a social drinker will become an alcoholic? Who knows when liquor will rob a man or woman of self respect, of family, of job, of all that is worthwhile in life, and leave him or her part of the flotsam of humanity?

In the February 1969 issue of "Today's Health,"

published by the American Medical Association, there appears a panel discussion by three eminent scholars, two of them psychiatrists and one an internist, all of them experts in the field of narcotics and alcohol.

The subject of the discussion was: "Should Children Be Taught to Drink?"

Incredible as it is that such a subject would even be considered for discussion in a respected medical journal, it is more unbelievable that these highly schooled experts would agree among themselves that children should be "introduced" to alcohol at an early age, probably as young as four.

All three experts were opposed to alcoholism and appeared earnestly to seek a way to abolish it, but none even suggested abstention.

They regarded alcohol as an essential part of modern life, such as automobiles, for example, and felt that people—even youngsters—should learn to handle their alcohol as they learn to handle their cars.

To the question: "Should children be taught about drinking?" one of the psychiatrists answered: "Yes, if they intend to be drinkers during their lives." He went on:

"All our teaching about alcohol is fear-oriented, full of horror stories about the evils of drink. If we are ever going to prevent alcoholism as an emotional illness, we need to develop healthy attitudes in people, starting when they are young."

The doctors admitted that alcoholism is bad and

that most alcoholics had alcoholic parents; that most drinkers started drinking in their homes by the time they were 14, and that they learned to drink from their parents.

Their main criticism was that when parents take a drink they do not do it "as a ritual," or make something "sacramental" out of it. They said that if parents would drink "culturally" in the home and teach their little ones to do likewise, there would be fewer alcoholics.

One of them recommended that this "ritual" with the children begin at about four years of age with diluted wine, which could be given less and less dilution as the children grew up. If drinking was "ritualistic," with "ceremony" and "culture" at the dinner table, extremes would be avoided and thus there would be fewer drunkards, it was said.

It seems unbelievable! But there was one thing they said that was easily understood, and that was an admission by the psychiatrist for the New York State Narcotics Commission:

"I also want to see that it ought to be clear that we are speaking largely from hypothesis. This is an educated guess, a calculated reasoning by people in the field. But it's far from scientifically proved or really firm."

Thank heaven for that admission!

Of course it is not scientific. Of course it is purely guesswork. But why do men of this standing in scientific circles advise parents to teach their children to drink

—if they do it "culturally" and with "ritual"—when they admit there is no scientific basis for such advice?

They may talk about not liking the horror stories accompanying reports on drinking, but those horror stories cannot be brushed aside.

It is still a fact that of every 50 cars approaching you on the highway, one is being driven by a person who is drunk—not just drinking—but drunk.

It is still a fact, as pointed out by the U.S. News and World Report, that drunken driving took 25,000 lives last year alone, and that there were 800,000 crashes due to alcohol in the nation last year.

It is also a fact that highway slaughter takes more lives and causes more injuries than all of our wars combined. Up to 1961 in America 1,375,000 persons were killed on highways, compared to 1,125,000 killed in all the wars in which we have ever been involved. These same wars listed 1,275,000 wounded, compared with 48,000,000 injured on the highways.

In Westchester County, N.Y., over an eight-year period 49 percent of all drivers in fatal single car accidents were drunk, and an additional 24 percent had been drinking but were not adjudged as drunk. In Montana 48 percent of all drivers killed in auto accidents were drunk. In Buffalo a check showed that 55 percent of all accidents involved liquor.

Why shouldn't we have horror stories about liquor?

How grateful the Latter-day Saints should be that more than a century ago, the Lord gave to them sound guidance on the matter of narcotics and stimulants.

As a word of wisdom, adapted to the capacity of the weakest among us, he said:

"And again, strong drinks are not for the belly." Can anyone misunderstand that language?

The merciful God, who is interested in sparing His children from the ills of narcotic influences, has given us sound advice to abstain. Do we have the faith and good judgment to obey Him?

How wise was the Lord when He said:

"In consequence of evils and designs which do and will exist in the hearts of conspiring men in the last days, I have warned you, and forewarn you, by giving unto you this word of wisdom by revelation—THAT INASMUCH AS ANY MAN DRINKETH WINE OR STRONG DRINK AMONG YOU, BEHOLD IT IS NOT GOOD, NEITHER MEET IN THE SIGHT OF YOUR FATHER."

How much longer will "self sufficient" man lean on his own wisdom and turn his back upon the Lord?

Chapter Eight

Tobacco Is Also Blamed

If you smoke tobacco, there is only one more step to smoking marijuana. And if you smoke marijuana it is but another short step to the heavier drugs and eventual destruction.

We do not suppose for a moment that all cigaret smokers become drug addicts, but what we do say is that if you smoke, you smoke, and it is easy to go from one form of smoking to another. That is what has happened to the so-called "hippie" element.

Many of them have drifted from long hair and tobacco to filthy clothes and marijuana, and from that to LSD and heroin and moral corruption.

It is all in one big package with them. Dare we emulate them?

It is not necessary here to review all of the medical reasons why tobacco is bad for man but we should recognize that if we smoke we lower the standards which help to prevent us from indulging in marijuana. If you don't smoke at all, you will not smoke marijuana either.

There are other things about smoking, too, that teenagers should recognize.

The Cowles Magazine and Broadcasting Company, one of the large institutions of the Middle West, publishes an "Insider's Newsletter" which said:

"STRAIGHT A's — All Up In Smoke.

"The idea of banning teen-age smoking won strong academic support this week from research that indicates smoking may or may not stunt your child's physical growth, but definitely does affect his brainpower.

"So say Dr. Eva Salber and a team of doctors at Harvard University, who have recently ended a study of smoking habits of 6,810 children between the seventh and twelfth grades. The burning conclusion: There is a strong relationship between achievement and abstinence from smoking. Those who don't smoke run rings around their classmates. The unfiltered facts:

"High school students who didn't smoke had higher IQs, did better consistently in school, went farther in their education than smokers. More non-smokers made the advanced studies.

"The student smokers who consumed less than a pack a week had higher IQs and grades than the heavier smokers.

"The difference between the non-smokers as far as

their academic studies were concerned was most striking among the boys."

Confirming this comes an article in the "Medical Reporter," which said:

"A report on 22,000 high school boys and girls in Portland, Oregon, indicates that heavy smokers are less likely to be good students than non-smokers.

"The study supervised by Dr. Daniel Horn turned up the following:

"More heavy smokers fall behind proper grade levels than non-smokers; they tend to take less challenging courses; they are more likely to end up at the bottom of the class.

"A similar study of 6,800 students in Newton, Massachusetts, high schools revealed in all grades, mean intelligence levels of children who did not smoke were higher than those of students who did smoke."

In a recent nationwide survey reported by Dr. Harold S. Diehl for the American Cancer Society, smoking fathers were asked: "Do you want your children to smoke?" Eighty percent replied with a positive "No."

And yet every day about 4,000 young people in America take their first cigaret. About half of the nation's teenagers are regular smokers by the time they are 18 years old. If the present trend continues, a million children now in school will die of lung cancer, and many times more this number will become disabled and die of coronary heart disease, emphysema or circulatory disease, all related to their smoking habits.

Tobacco Is Also Blamed

The U.S. Surgeon General's Office reports that each year in this country:

Smoking causes between 125,000 and 300,000 premature deaths.

Three hundred thousand coronary attacks.

Two million cases of chronic bronchitis or emphysema.

Two million cases of sinusitis.

One million cases of peptic ulcers.

The schools of the nation are taking up the project of urging the teenagers in high school particularly to refuse to take up smoking.

They are using filmstrips and specially prepared educational kits to show the students the great danger of smoking.

Said the New York Times concerning this program:

"Among the items being distributed is a chart bearing the legend:

"What are your chances of getting lung cancer? It depends on how much and how long you have smoked. Half a pack of cigarettes a day? Your risk goes up eight times. Two packs or more? Twenty times greater.

"Schools in many parts of the country are cooperating in bringing this material to the attention of students, according to the society. Often this is done through lectures given by the science teachers with the aid of the film strip. It was said that the New York City Board of Education had tentatively agreed to help by furnishing mailing lists covering schools in the area.

"The kits for distribution in Manhattan and the

Bronx contain batches of material earmarked for students, teachers and administrators, custodial workers and parents. The society is also willing to furnish a lecturer, projector and projectionist.

"By working through the schools and through youth groups such as the Boy Scouts, it is hoped to persuade a large proportion of the nation's young people that smoking may lead to lung cancer.

"In Manhattan and the Bronx alone, special kits were sent to 1,500 public, private and parochial schools. In the first eight months of the campaign, more than 10,000 film strips on the subject have been distributed throughout the country.

"The program involves a sizable portion of the Cancer Society's budget for educational activities, plus outlays by local cancer committees. It is clearly designed to offset efforts of cigarette makers to sell their products to young persons."

For the Latter-day Saints, the path of safety again lies in keeping the Lord's commandments. The Word of Wisdom truly is WISDOM.

Chapter Nine

Morals Are Involved

"Like begets like" is an old saying, and yet so true.

Drug addiction, liquor and tobacco are evils which beckon to other evils, and involve their victims in almost every kind of sin, one of the worst of which is immorality.

Let's talk frankly about sex. What is it? And what is it for? Who made it?

It was God who made sex, and he did so to help us become co-creators with him.

The bringing forth of life is a sacred matter, because it is part of God's work, and he is the personification of purity.

The purpose of sex is reproduction of the species. If it were not for that, there would be no need for sex. And of course without it there would be no life, because if life is to continue, it must reproduce itself.

God made all things, all forms of life. The vegetable kingdom reproduces itself after its own kind. Is there any evidence of a deviation in its reproduction pattern? Of course not. To raise the question seems ridiculous. All the lower forms of life follow a particular pattern of reproduction. It is God's pattern, which he laid out for them in the beginning. And it is all "good," as he expressed it in Genesis.

Let us consider the animal kingdom. It too reproduces itself. It has higher intelligence, with what seems to be some power of choice. For example, a dog will obey or disobey its master. A horse may elect to "throw" a rider at a rodeo.

Every animal has the power of reproduction. But does anyone see an animal using its sex improperly? Again the question seems ridiculous. And yet, animals do have some intelligence. They do have instinct or intelligence in using their sex for reproduction. But do they abuse their sex? Has anyone ever seen an animal abuse its sex?

God set the limitations within which animals, like plants, reproduce, and they invariably stay within the limits God set for them. Should not humans do as well?

Think about it for a moment, and ask yourselves if we should not be higher and better than animals. Should humans abuse their ability to reproduce? Should we debase it as a source of entertainment?

Sex is sacred and was made for a sacred purpose. God commands mankind to multiply and replenish the

Morals Are Involved

earth. But as is the case with the vegetable and the animal kingdoms, he expects it to be done in his own way. And his own way for humans is within the virtuous and chaste order of marriage. This is the limitation he placed on human reproduction.

In God's plan, there should be no sex activity for humans outside of marriage. God ordained marriage, according to the scripture, and it was He who provided that only within that sacred order should we reproduce ourselves.

Outside of marriage, sex association becomes adulterous and vicious, and is condemned by the Lord as a miscarriage of his divine plans.

If we truly believe in God, we will obey his law of chastity.

President David O. McKay at one time said:

"He who is unchaste in young manhood is untrue to a trust given to him by the parents of the girl, and she who is unchaste in maidenhood is untrue to her future husband and lays the foundation of unhappiness, suspicion and discord in the home. Do not worry about these teachers who have much to say about inhibitions. Keep in mind this eternal truth, that chastity is a virtue to be prized as one of life's noblest achievements. It is the crowning virtue of womanhood, and every redblooded man knows that this is true."

President Joseph F. Smith said at one time: "No more loathsome cancer disfigures the body and soul of society today than the frightful affliction of sexual sin.

It vitiates the very fountains of life and bequeaths its foul effects to the yet unborn as a legacy of death."

Chastity is indeed a divine law of God. It was given anciently to Moses, it was re-stated by the Savior in his day, and has been announced once again in modern times through the Prophet Joseph Smith.

Sex is not for illicit entertainment. It is not for the unmarried. It is to be preserved in its purity even as life itself.

Its abuse brings heartbreak, disillusionment and dreadful diseases.

Chapter Ten

The Wages of Sin

The Chicago Tribune recently quoted Dr. Norman J. Rose, head of epidemiology for the Illinois Department of Public Health, as saying:

"Contrary to the popular notion that venereal disease is no longer a menace, the U.S. Public Health Service reports that VD IS THE NATION'S LEADING COMMUNICABLE DISEASE."

Publications of the U.S. Department of Public Health confirm this and say that only the common cold is more widespread in America than venereal disease.

Because of the moral breakdown that has come over the world, promiscuity is spreading rapidly among the young adults and teenagers of the nation.

A direct result is that there are about 1,500 new cases of venereal disease among the youth of the nation every day.

Drugs, Drinks & Morals

There is no vaccine that will prevent it.

Only one thing can stop it, and that is chastity.

In Atlanta, Georgia, is located the nation's communicable disease center. There many top doctors are studying this problem every day. Every disease comes under intense scrutiny.

There are two kinds of venereal disease, and both of them are rampant.

And why are they rampant? Because young people in particular have become so lax in their morals that they indulge frequently in pre-marital sex, as they call it. Fornication is what the scriptures call it.

Venereal disease is so easily contracted through physical relationships that it spreads with little restraint. Most young people are afraid to have treatment. They are frightened of their parents and also of their doctors. They apparently would rather suffer and spread the disease to others than to seek medical aid or repent and abstain from sin.

The Atlanta Journal and Constitution recently sent a top reporter to interview officials at the communicable disease center. It afterward carried a full-page article under the title: "Stop Snickering, VD can kill you." Among other things it reported:

"THE CASES INVOLVE CHILDREN, TEEN-AGERS AND SOMETIMES ENTIRE FAMILIES.

"FOR EXAMPLE:

"An 11-year-old boy walked into the health department, alone, and said he thought he had gonorrhea.

TABLE XI PRIMARY AND SECONDARY SYPHILIS CASE RATES PER 100,000 POPULATION – FISCAL YEAR 1967

Case Rate	No. of States
0 – 1.9	8
2 – 3.9	13
4 – 9.9	14
10 – 19.9	10
20 – 76.3	6

Drugs, Drinks & Morals

"After an examination confirmed his suspicions, the epidemiologist, a specialist in tracking communicable diseases, discreetly asked the name of his girl friend.

"SHE WAS NINE YEARS OLD. When she was brought into the clinic for treatment, she said she had made a 'bargain' with the little boy for a dollar.

"SINCE THE BARGAIN WITH HIM, SHE HAD 'SOLD' TO FOUR OTHER BOYS FOR THE SAME AMOUNT.

"WHEN AN EIGHT-YEAR-OLD GIRL CAME TO THE HEALTH DEPARTMENT WITH SYPHILIS, SHE NAMED SEVERAL BOYS, AGES 8, 9 AND 10, WITH WHOM SHE HAD HAD SEXUAL CONTACT.

"An official took the child home and asked her parents whether they knew anybody in the neighborhood WHO HAD A RASH.

" 'I DO,' HER MOTHER RESPONDED, HOLDING OUT HER HANDS, PALMS UP. THE PALMS WERE BLOTCHED WITH A RASH INDICATIVE OF SECONDARY SYPHILIS.

"THE LITTLE GIRL'S FATHER SAID HE HAD HAD A RASH SIMILAR TO HIS WIFE'S, BUT IT WAS GONE NOW.

"These cases came from lower-class homes, but health officials emphasize that VD IS NOT A DISEASE OF THE POOR.

"A businessman from a fashionable Northside neighborhood attended an out-of-town convention and returned with primary syphilis.

"When he came to the health department, he was beside himself with fear of losing his job, his wife, and his reputation."

It is reported that whereas everyone knows when they become infected with syphilis, with gonorrhea it is different. Women particularly do not know when they become infected with gonorrhea, and unknowingly can pass it on to their little babies or to older children, even by using the same towel. It can be transmitted by using the same lipstick as an infected person, or through kissing.

One official of the center in Atlanta said: "The only disease more common in the United States than VD is the common cold, and there is no immunizing agent against it."

The center reports that from syphilis alone there are more than 3,000 deaths a year, and that many more are caused by this disease but that syphilis is not mentioned in the death certificate. Some believe the true death rate is nearer 12,000 a year.

Further complicating the gonorrhea control problem, the gonococcus germ is growing more resistant to penicillin and the antibiotics so effective in the past.

New strains from foreign countries, especially Southeast Asia, are showing strong resistance.

Most young people receive no treatment for this disease and when they go untreated, not only do they spread it to their friends, but they bring frightening effects upon their own health.

Drugs, Drinks & Morals

Gonorrhea causes blindness to newborn babies, and results in crippling arthritis and heart disease in persons infected.

Syphilis, in addition to being a killer, can be passed on to unborn children, causing them to be born deaf or blind or retarded or dead. A MOTHER WITH SYPHILIS HAS ONLY ONE CHANCE IN SIX OF HAVING A HEALTHY BABY.

One of the truly frightening things about this disease is that it may erupt from five to twenty years after infection, and even at that late date it can cause blindness, insanity, heart disease, paralysis or deformity, the latter usually through arthritic-like conditions.

Official reports show that in the calendar year 1966 the rate of infectious syphilis among teenagers (15-19) was 22.5 per 100,000 of total population, or more than twice the national rate of 10.9 for all age groups.

Gonorrhea among teenagers reached a rate of 424.9 per 100,000 of total population, while the national rate was 178.6 for all age groups. The rate of increase was higher in this age group than in any others.

There was an increase of 20.2 percent of gonorrhea cases among teenagers in 1967 over 1966, as against an increase of 15 percent for the entire nation.

Based on reported cases only, the ratio of gonorrhea infection among teenagers in 1967 was one to every 200, and for young men and young women in the 20-24-year age group the ratio was one in every 100 for that particular year.

The Wages of Sin

Utah is one of the cleaner states in the union in regard to venereal infection. In this state the rate for syphilis is only 10.2 per 100,000 of population. Some other states are: Arizona, 52; Delaware, 105; District of Columbia, 260; Illinois, 63; Maryland, 87; New York, 82.

In gonorrhea cases the rate for Utah is 89 per 100,000 of population. Idaho is 115 and Arizona is 207. But in the District of Columbia it is 1544; in Illinois, 363; Maryland, 240; New York, 219.

Figures sometimes do not portray the real picture. A 1969 report says that one in every 30 Americans 20 to 24 years of age has VD. This includes reported cases as well as an estimate of unreported cases. Think of this condition in terms of smallpox or polio. What if one in every 30 such persons in America had polio? What if that number had smallpox? What if that many had to be operated on for cancer? Wouldn't we be shaken by the very thought of it? Yet that is the condition in regard to VD.

Latter-day Saints at least should know the true meaning of virtue. God's word is never passé. It is never outdated. No matter what the philosophies of men may be, God's word—for Latter-day Saints—must prevail.

No man on earth can ever cancel out the divine injunction:

"THOU SHALT NOT COMMIT ADULTERY."

Chapter Eleven

Ever Hear of Chastity?

Parade Magazine, published as a Sunday supplement in many American newspapers, recently carried an article on illegitimacy.

The author reported that in the United States there is a steadily growing number of illegitimate births among teenagers. He said, in fact, that there are 18 illegitimate mothers aged 15 to 19 for every 1,000 of that age group in the nation.

This is appalling, especially when it is realized that the birthrate for the United States as a whole is 17.8 per thousand of total population, and that this figure includes legitimate as well as illegitimate births.

But even this is no measure of the amount of promiscuity practiced by teenagers in the nation, for all who are involved in this tragedy do not have babies.

The author rightfully mentions that the cost of this

illegitimacy in money is tremendous to the taxpayers, because a high percentage of children thus born are placed on public welfare.

But then the author says: "At this moment there are 145,000 known unwed mothers in that particular age group (15 to 19) with their illegitimacy rate steadily rising."

And he adds: "It is going up because these school-age girls are woefully ignorant of birth control information, so ignorant and uneducated in that area that they continue to bear children out of wedlock, even though they don't want to."

In defense of this peculiar position, he says that the illegitimacy rate among non-whites is 80.2 per thousand in the 15 to 19 age group as compared to 9.0 for the whites, and then goes on to say that both whites and non-whites even among the highly educated are incredibly ignorant when "it comes to practical sex information."

In other words, he seems to point out that the only thing wrong with all this illegitimacy is that girls don't have sense enough to prevent the birth of these unfortunate and unwanted babies.

Has he ever heard of the law of chastity?

Is America to accept fornication as a way of life, and weep only over the birth of illegitimates because girls are not fed birth control information and pills it recommends?

This sort of talk is put into the hands of both girls

and boys by newspaper publishers, as though themselves endorsed such wickedness!

The answer is not "the pill." The answer is a return to chastity.

"The pill" will never prevent promiscuity. It leads to it and invites it. And neither can "the pill" prevent the epidemic of venereal disease that is now rampant in the world.

Some girls suppose that their fornication is not as sinful if they do not become pregnant, but this is a false notion.

Illicit sex sin is adulterous whether or not there is a pregnancy.

And taking "the pill" in no way lessens the seriousness of the sin.

Takers of "the pill" too must remember that it cannot be taken without risk to health and even life. Many women still die from its side effects. The "pill" is far from safe.

It is appalling that it is officially estimated that 1,500 teenagers catch VD every day in the United States, and that an additional 1,300 adults do likewise.

Officials point out that one of the frightening dangers in this condition is the most VD is not reported nor is it treated. Doctors are required by law to report all VD cases that come under their care.

But teenagers particularly do not report their infection, and as a result receive no treatment. Yet they continue to indulge in promiscuity, and as they do so

Ever Hear of Chastity?

—as carriers—they transmit the disease to others with whom they associate in sin.

Or does America no longer regard it as sin?

Most people will remember:

> "Sin is a monster of such dreadful mein
> That to be hated needs but to be seen.
> But seen too oft, familiar with her face,
> First we pity, then endure, then embrace."

Public acceptance is certainly a fickle thing, as the verse indicates.

One businessman recently said, "You know—miniskirts—you hardly notice them any more. They are just a part of today's living."

And how horrified people were when they first came out! "First we pity, then endure, then embrace."

It is the same with adulterous relationships. They surely were considered as "a monster of dreadful mein," and the "Scarlet Letter" was certainly applied to guilty parties in the past, if caught.

But now? How many make fornication a part of every date? It is said that this is the case on certain college campuses.

The very fact that a newpaper columnist would fail to lament the act, but only feel sorry for a poor distribution of "the pill," is evidence of what we say here.

It is past time to return to chastity. We must stop every influence which tears it down!

Every home in America must look to its standards.

Parents as well as children must take a new firm stand for virtue. Unless we do, the time will come when America as we know it will disappear.

Chapter Twelve

Dress and Morality

There is a definite relationship between styles of dress and morality. This has been established through studies that have been made in schools, in reformatories and in other groups.

Modesty is one of the chief bastions of virtue, both for men and for women.

We cannot expose our person without creating lust in someone's mind if not in our own.

We cannot lay claim to virtue if we violate the very basis upon which it rests.

How short are skirts when they are too short?

How tight are skirts or slacks when they are too tight?

Should the physical form ever be exhibited to the public eye?

Every young person must come to realize that virtue

is more important than styles and that goodness far outweighs popularity in importance and value.

If we are to be Latter-day Saints in very deed, how will we dress? Is it all-important to be like other people, no matter how extreme they may become?

Do we please the boys when we are immodest? Do we please the other girls? Do we please anyone?

There is a "Girlwatchers" club at the Lakeside Junior High School in San Diego. It has a membership of 39 boys.

Near the close of the last semester of school, the club published and distributed to all girls on the campus the following proclamation:

"We, the boys of the Girlwatchers Club, have been watching girls for the past four weeks. Some of what we have observed has pleased us. But, much of what we have seen displeased, disgusted and repulsed us.

"Therefore, we have agreed and resolved that some changes must be made. We feel that changes suggested are reasonable and fair. In general all we are asking is the girls again become feminine in their thoughts, words and deeds, because they should be different from boys.

"We are tired of constantly being forced to look at girls' underwear. For example: Pettipants hanging out; skirts not long enough to cover underwear during such normal activities as sitting, stooping, reaching up or running.

"Boys do not like the carelessness girls display when sitting with legs apart or lying on floors, grass, benches

Dress and Morality

and retaining walls, constantly making others look at their underwear. This is no thrill for boys or anyone else—just obnoxious!

"We are disturbed by girls who wear improper hose. Too many are wearing hose not long enough. The viewer is greeted by the unlovely sight of hose tops, garters and bulging thighs all hanging below skirts. Ugh!

"We find girls draped in boys' or men's clothing unattractive and unfeminine. Many are wearing sailors' pea-jackets, boys' shirts with tails hanging out . . . and sundry other items of male clothing. Wear your own clothes and let us wear ours.

"We have been badly frightened too many times by girls who use makeup with little or no skill or even good sense. It is hideous! . . . Use a little makeup, learn how to apply it. . . .

"We are concerned about girls' choice of vocabulary in both spoken and written communication. We take a dim view of girls using both profane and obscene language in their conversations with each other and with us. . . . Clean up your mouths or keep quiet.

"We think girls passing notes or letters around is silly, but girls passing obscene or vulgar notes is revolting and intolerable. Stop writing dirty notes—period!

"We are concerned about the large number of girls whose general behavior is becoming increasingly unfeminine and boylike.

"Girls who greet us by pushing us, hitting us, pounding us on the back, chasing us or mussing up our hair or clothing leave us absolutely cold. Try just saying hello. . . .

"Girls who ask us if we love them, if we'll go steady with them, or if we'll date them are nowhere." (In kid slang, "nowhere" indicates a loser.) "If we want to be with you, we'll let you know. Don't call us, we'll call you!

"Girls who run everywhere all day and who come out in skirts at noon and try to play basketball or football with boys turn us off. Girl athletes are great, but pay attention to time, place and costume.

"Girls who smoke, ditch (cut classes), shoplift and hitch-hike are well known to all of us and respected by NONE of us. Suggestion: Don't smoke; attend school, pay for the things you need and walk where you are going."

The "proclamation" concluded with an announcement that girls failing to comply with it would be subjected to "a total boycott of all friendly relations" with the 39 boys.

In fact, the boycott started with the posting of the proclamation on a school bulletin board Friday morning. The circular was produced, distributed and posted with hearty approval of the school principal, John Westrick, and boys' counselor, Larry Schreiner.

"The Girlwatchers Club started five weeks ago," Schreiner recalled. "It has no officers, just the 39 boys who belong.

"All girls got a copy of the proclamation in the

home rooms Friday morning and they all froze. They were still sore all day Monday, but by Tuesday they showed so much improvement, particularly in connection with underwear, the boycott was lifted pending a Girl-watchers' meeting Friday."

Chapter Thirteen

Protective Commandments

The all-seeing eye of the Lord foresaw the evils which would afflict mankind, and to help us avoid many pitfalls, he gave us protective commandments.

Each commandment was intended to shield us from harm and evil, and to increase our ability to grow and develop under the direction of the Spirit of the Lord.

What are some of these protective commandments?

One of the first that always comes to mind is the Word of Wisdom, since tobacco, liquor and other such substances are now under such persistent attack by both scientists and the governments of various lands.

Evidence brought to light by researchers proves beyond any doubt the foresight of the Lord as he said:

"In consequence of the evils and designs which do and will exist in the hearts of conspiring men in the last days, I have warned you, and forewarn you, by giving unto you this word of wisdom by revelation."

The American Medical Association Bulletin on Tobacco, Volume 7, Number 2, showed once again how certain "conspiring men" are seeking to set at naught the efforts of doctors and other scientists in protecting the nation against the evils of tobacco smoking.

Bills in Congress which would require warning labels on all cigarets are being weakened so that they become meaningless, doctors point out in disgust.

The tobacco industry is using millions of dollars to protect itself from legislation which they know would reduce their sales.

To combat this contrary move, many physicians all over the nation are communicating with their congressmen to reassure them of the medical evidence on the risks of smoking.

Many doctors are putting pressure on hospitals to ban the sale of cigarets in these institutions. It is well known what a battle is on to wipe out advertising of tobacco on television and radio and in published periodicals.

The liquor industry is making an all-out effort to persuade young people to begin to drink, just as the cigaret companies are trying to induce every child to begin to smoke. It is a "conspiracy" in reality, as the Lord said in the revelation. Hence the protective commandment.

The Prophet Joseph Smith interpreted the "hot drinks" in the Word of Wisdom to mean tea and coffee. Present-day research on these drinks is now showing that they contain substances, in addition to the usually mentioned caffeine, which are very detrimental to health. One researcher said that within ten years the medical pressure against the use of tea and coffee will be as great as is the present effort against tobacco.

What is another protective commandment? We must hasten to mention it: "Thou shalt not commit adultery."

When it is realized that venereal disease is second only to the common cold in its extensiveness in America, we began to understand what a protection the law of chastity really is. And when we realize that VD brings death, blindness, insanity, heart problems, and crippling disease, we understand even better the Lord's wisdom in warning us.

What a protective commandment the Golden Rule is—if it were only kept!

If everyone did to others as he would be done by, if everyone loved his neighbor as himself, we would have heaven on earth. We would have no more wars, no more divorces, no more crime, none of the numerous other personal ills that afflict us.

Thou shalt not steal, thou shalt not lie, thou shalt not covet—mention any of the Ten Commandments, and what do you have? The means of self protection from the ills of the world.

Honor thy father and thy mother—how wonderfully that law would heal the wounds of disrupted families!

The law of tithing is a protective commandment, if any is. It protects us economically as nothing else can do.

And so we might go on. God's laws are all *protective* in the manner in which they assist us to develop, and as they preserve us from the ills of the world.

Let us not set them aside for any false security the world can offer.

Chapter Fourteen

Avoid Pornography

One of the worst attacks upon good morals in the world today comes in the form of pornography.

It is seen on the screen in an advanced stage, as well as in many a printed page.

Why should any Latter-day Saint youth debase himself with pornography?

Smut is regarded by J. Edgar Hoover, head of the FBI, as one of the leading cause of many kinds of crime.

Recently he said:

"The publication and sale of obscene material is BIG business in America today. Degenerate sex pictures and pornographic literature, covertly peddled and sold in most cities and communities, net greedy smut merchants millions of dollars annually.

"It is impossible to estimate the amount of harm to impressionable teen-agers and to assess the volume of sex crimes attributable to pornography, but its influence is extensive.

"Sexual violence is increasing at an alarming pace. Many parents are deeply concerned about conditions which involve young boys and girls in sex parties and illicit relations.

"While there is no official yardstick with which to measure accurately the reasons for increases in any criminal violation, we must face reality.

"Pornography, in all its forms, is one major cause of sex crimes, sexual aberrations and perversions.

"Is our society becoming so wicked that we are turning from virtue and integrity to immorality and degradation? Are we becoming morally bankrupt and letting our principles of conduct and decency deteriorate? Are we forsaking the simple teachings of right over wrong and good over bad?

"Let us look about us. In the publishing, theatrical and entertainment fields, are the good, enlightening and educational qualities of their products being overshadowed by too much emphasis on obscenity, vulgarity, incest and homosexuality?

"Many people believe this to be true. But the legitimate productions of these media are rather mild when compared with the 'hard core' pornography flooding the country in the forms of film, 'playing' cards, 'comic' books, paperbacks and pictures.

"Such filth in the hands of young people and curious adolescents does untold damage and leads to disastrous consequences.

"Police officials who have discussed this critical problem with me unequivocally state that lewd and obscene material plays a motivating role in sexual violence."

As is pointed out by this great advocate of law and order, "Pornography in all its forms is one major cause of sex crimes."

We have pornographic films, pornographic advertising, pornographic magazines, books and posters, and shops which specialize in these things. Public newsstands are full of it.

Styles, both of men and women, have become largely pornographic. Tight, revealing clothing is as disgusting on men as it is on women. Shorter and shorter skirts are pornographic in the extreme.

All have their effect in boosting the sex crime now engulfing our nation and the world. And these are given further impetus by the demoralizing effect of liquor, now so freely and easily made available.

In some of the best residential areas of our cities, people are frightened to walk alone at night, and particularly are girls and women not safe. Why? Who are the attackers? The sex deviates!

And why are there so many sex deviates?

Because perversion is made *popular* by what we read and see and buy.

The following stimulating editorial was published recently by the Sacramento (California) Union. It so effectively sets forth one of America's greatest dangers that we reproduce it entirely below.

Avoid Pornography

Entitled "Moral Decay Stench Getting Even Riper," the editorial says:

"Moral decay is as unwelcome in our society as any disease. Yet it is an unwholesome and all-too-common sight today. It is visible, in all its evil degradation, in almost every aspect of life and communications.

"In public and in private, there are few activities which have not been seduced by a permissive environment. This has unhappily led to promotion and acceptance of standards which bring out in man all that leads to excess and indulgence.

"Good taste is rudely brushed aside. The senses, which were made for the fulfillment and enjoyment of things which are beautiful, are tempted to become abused and depraved.

"There is a subversive pretense to be educational, entertaining, and instructive. The moral junk which fills so much of what is offered for reading, hearing, or viewing is an insult. It is an affront to the very spirit and meaning of man's highest endeavors.

"Instead of using the precious gifts of communication for man's betterment and true happiness, we find them overflowing with the decadence of gutter filth.

"Instead of aiming always to achieve excellence and toward helping mankind, there are those who prey like vultures on a public unfortunately only too ready to sink into the contaminated, polluted atmosphere of depravity.

"The poison of pornography is as great a menace

to society today as the growing crime rate with which it is so often associated.

"From books, movies, magazines, shows, and meetings there is an overwhelming abundance of encouragement to lower standards. It is made attractive to sink into the 'accepted' and depraved ways of the pornographic promoters.

"There is so-called 'pop' art, which often is simply an excuse for utter vulgarity. There are 'love-ins,' which are euphemistic cloaks for immorality.

"On all sides we are experiencing the spread of gutter filth which is passed off as 'literature.' It seduces the young and makes a mockery of the fine art of literary expression. The four-letter words and the concentration on deviant sex are excused on grounds of realism.

"Even the beauty of the ballet has been disfigured with portrayals which break the bounds of decency and make a mockery of this beautifully expressive art form.

"Movies, radio, and television, whose mass visual and audio communication should cause producers to ponder their effects, are not innocent. More and more movies stretch to the utmost the limits of decency. And sexual perverts have been featured on both radio and television as interesting interview personalities.

"We are assuredly at war today on the home front. It is a war to fight against the insidious evil of 'anything goes.' We must re-establish moral codes and endorse them, before everything good is gone."

Chapter Fifteen

We Have a Destiny!

Humanity will rise or fall through its attitude toward the law of chastity. If the world will honor virtue, it can expect to receive God's blessings, but if it persists in the practice of sodomy, adultery, and other perversions, it can expect only destruction, for the wage of sin is death.

It is this awesome fact that should frighten at least the Christian world into a realization that we are being hurled into an abyss of moral degradation. The so-called sex revolution can destroy us.

As people change their standards of right and wrong, they begin to suppose that what was sin a generation ago is no longer so, that standards are relative things which may be altered at will through usage and desire, and that old-fashioned goodness now has turned into priggishness.

Many actually seem to think that the popular trend is what determines right or wrong, and that moral values change with public sentiment.

A mother recently wrote to a medical doctor who conducts a newspaper column and asked whether she should provide her daughter with a supply of "the pill" as she left to attend a boarding school. In writing to the doctor, the mother said:

"Personally I don't approve of sexual relations outside of marriage, but I wonder if I should be realistic and supply my daughter with birth control pills, just in case."

Can any mother in her right mind take such a position? Has the writer of this letter never taught her daughter the Lord's law of chastity? Why does she dread pregnancy but apparently have no great aversion to her daughter's loss of virtue?

Was this girl never taught about her bodily functions in the sanctity of a good home?

We are not animals, to dwell only in a physical world. We are the offspring of God, learning in this life to become like him.

He decreed that human beings never shall indulge in sex outside of holy matrimony, which he himself instituted.

This is his definition of chastity. This is what he requires of every man and every woman.

This is why—on the fiery slopes of Mt. Sinai—he declared:

We Have a Destiny

"Thou shalt not commit adultery."

This is why, in his Sermon on the Mount, the Savior taught that anyone who even looks upon another with lust has committed adultery in his heart.

Some people justify their immorality by saying that restrictions against it are merely religious rules which have no meaning any longer because there really isn't any God.

Thoughtful people now recognize the existence of Deity more than ever before. Persons of genuine intellect, the true researchers, the great philosophers and the outstanding educators not only acknowledge him but they also worship him.

It is the selfish element in the world which no longer accepts Deity. And why? Because they do not want to be interrupted in their ingrown pursuits and are so involved in their personal desires, passions, appetites and lusts, that they have no room left for sacred things. Therefore, in their selfishness they reject or ignore God.

To the true realist, God is a significant Presence who guides the ultimate destiny of the world. But let us never forget that one of his most basic laws concerns morality.

That law is irrevocable and inescapable and applies to all, whether we believe in God or not. Everyone is subject to its penalties no matter how they may try to ignore them. The wage of sin is death—even to the unbeliever!

Immorality is next to murder in God's category of crime and always brings in its wake both destruction

Drugs, Drinks & Morals

and remorse, even to college students who carry the pill with a mother's consent.

This nation was built upon a foundation of morality and spirituality. It is just possible that a rejection of these basic factors may bring about its fall. It was so with Greece and Rome. It can happen to us unless we repent.

Every one of us would do well to remember that the "mills of the Gods grind slowly, but they grind exceeding small."

No one can flout the divine law with impunity.

Every right-thinking person should be willing even to die if necessary in defense of virtue, whether that death be physical or social.

"Thou shalt not commit adultery" will forever stand as an immutable law to all human beings. This generation may rationalize itself into complete intoxication with sin and proclaim to high heaven that it is old fashioned to be clean, but it will yet wake up to the stern reality that God does not change and that the moral laws are his and not man's to shift with every whim.

Adultery is still next to murder in the Lord's category of crime.

Homosexuality was made a capital crime in the Bible.

It was the Almighty who decreed that men and women must cover their nakedness by wearing proper clothing.

No amount of rationalizing can change God's law. No amount of fashion designing can turn immodesty into virtue and no amount of popularity can change sin into righteousness.

Once again we Latter-day Saints affirm the reality of the existence of Jesus Christ. Once again, as his humble servants, we define his law of personal purity and solemnly declare that sex sin is an abomination in the sight of God.

No one on earth can ever cancel the divine command which says "Thou shalt not commit adultery."

Apostasy from Christ through immorality is at least as bad as returning to paganism.

In this modern day, God has restored his pure gospel and his divine Church. Again he teaches the truth about himself and the way to come back into his presence.

Part of that restoration is a re-statement of the moral law.

Again comes his precept, commanding: "Be ye clean that bear the vessels of the Lord."

Again he appeals for virtue—complete, chaste, unblemished purity—on the part of his followers, for no unclean thing can come into his presence.

Virtue is as much a part of the restored gospel as baptism and the resurrection.

Chastity is as vital to us as the law and the prophets.

The work of God cannot abide in the midst of iniquity.

His people must not partake of the sins of Babylon or they will cease to be his people. Although we are in the world, we cannot indulge in its corruption.

We Latter-day Saints have a great modern message. We announce that God has appeared in our day. He has raised up modern prophets, like unto Moses, who speak for him.

He has established his Church again in this generation.

He is rearing a new and modern people—a priestly nation—a people of virtue and purity.

We have hundreds of thousands of youth in this heaven-blessed Church who love the restored truth.

But they must know that this truth includes virtue as well as worship, and that there can be no true worship without chastity.

With all our souls we appeal to the youth of Zion.

Believe with all your hearts in the restored gospel as given us through the Prophet Joseph Smith.

Believe that this restored gospel is the way of truth and joy.

Know that wickedness never was happiness, but that obedience and chastity lead to the abundant life.

Know that virtue is a vital part of the restored gospel and never can be separated from it.

Know and understand that no man or set of men, whether clergymen, educators, or government officials, can change divine law. They are neither greater nor more intelligent than the Almighty.

The Lord asks you to be as clean as he is, so that you may be fit to enter into his presence and become like him, for that is your destiny.

Index

Adultery, commandment on, 64, 73; see also chastity, immorality, sex

Alcohol, 21-24, 25-28; and cocktail parties, 22; and crime, 29; and dating, 23; and driving, 34; and drug addiction, 13; cost of, 25; effects of, 30-31; moral issue, 27; percent of nondrinkers, 22; studies of students, 24; teaching children to drink, 32

American Cancer Society, survey on smoking, 38

American Medical Association, report on tobacco, 63

Associated Press, report on Diane Linkletter, 6; figures on childbirth and drugs, 11; interview with Art Linkletter, 6-9; report on alcohol, drugs, venereal diseases, mental illness, 12

Atlanta Journal and Constitution, report on venereal disease, 46

Birthrate, illigitimate children, 52-53

Chastity, and illigitimate birthrate, 52-53; and pornography, 67-68; and venereal disease, 46; appeal for, 76; divine law of God, 44, 51, 53, 55, 71-73, 75, 76; preserving, 20, 72; statement by David O. McKay, 43; statement by Joseph F. Smith, 43

Cocktail parties, 22, 23

Coffee and Word of Wisdom, 63

Commandments, protective, 62-65

Cowles Magazine and Broadcasting Company, study on teenagers and smoking, 37

Crime, and alcohol, 29-30

Department of Health, Education and Welfare, 8

Dress, and pornography, 68; standards of, 57-61, 74

Drinking, and driving, 34; and teenagers, 25-26, 32-33; in home, 26; Methodists, 26; see also liquor

Drugs, and mental health, 11; Diane Linkletter death from, 1-4; effects of, 13-16, 17-19; effects on childbirth, 11; "turn on," 10-16; see also LSD, heroin, marijuana

Drunken driving figures on, 34

Emphysema, and tobacco, 38-39

Fort Worth, Texas, drug center, 18

Girl Watchers Club of San Diego, statement on dress, 58-61
Golden Rule, protective commandment, 64
Gonorrhea, case of 11-year-old boy, 46; physical effects of, 50; rate increasing, 12, 50-51; see also venereal disease
Grant, Heber J., story about banker and drinker, 22

Heart disease, and tobacco, 38-39
Heroin, addiction to, 14, 36; cost of, 18; effects of, 15, 17-18; smuggling of, 18
Homosexuality, crime of, 74
Hoover, J. Edgar, statement on pornography, 66
Hospitals, treatment for drug addiction, 11, 18
House Appropriations Subcommittee, testimony on drugs, 12-13

Immorality, 41-44; see also chastity, sex
IQ, effects of smoking on, 37

Klein, David, quotation on drinking, 21

Latter-day Saints, belief on alcohol, 22, 27-28, 35; gospel plan for clarity of mind, 19; publisher at cocktail party, 23; standards on chastity, 51, 75; Word of Wisdom, 35; see also commandments
Leary, Timothy, 8
Lexington, Kentucky, drug center, 18
Linkletter, Art, 1, 3, 4, 5-9; Diane, 1-6
Liquor, and pornography, 68; efforts of liquor industry, 63; Word of Wisdom, 62; see also drinking
LSD, and Diane Linkletter, 2, 5; number of users falling off, 12; see also drugs
Lung cancer and smoking, 38, 39, 40

Marijuana, addiction, 13; effects of, 14; habit forming, 11; tobacco leads to, 36; see also drugs
Marriage, and sex, 43, 72; ordained of God, 43
McKay, David O., statement on chastity, 43
Medical Reporter, article on teenagers and smoking, 38
Mental health and drugs, 11
Methodists, and drinking, 26
Modesty, see dress standards
Morals, 41-44

Index

Narcotics, see drugs, heroin, marijuana
New York Times report on teenage smoking, 39
Nondrinkers, 24, 25-23; percentages of, 25

Parents, commandment to honor, 64
Permissiveness, of society, 6
"Pill," birth control, 54, 72
Pornography, 66-70; statement by J. Edgar Hoover, 66
Pusher, drug, 14

Rose, Norman J., statement on venereal disease, 45

Sacramento Union, editorial on pornography, 68-70
Seliger, Robert V., interview on drug addiction, 13-16, 17
Seventeen magazine, article on drinking, 21
Sex, and pornography, 68; in animals, 42; purpose of, 41-42; sacredness of, 42; see also chastity, immorality
Smith, Joseph F., statement on chastity, 43
Smoking, see tobacco
Spirituality, nation built on, 74
Standards appeal for living of, 76; changing, 71; dress, 57-61
Syphilis, deaths from, 49; physical effects of, 50; rate of, 50-51

Tea, and Word of Wisdom, 63
Ten Commandments, 64
Tithing, protective commandment, 64
Today's Health, article on drinking, 32
Tobacco, 36-40; American Cancer Society study on, 38; American Medical Association report on, 63; and Word of Wisdom, 62; effects of, 38-39; fight against, 39; study of smoking habits of teenagers, 37-38

U.S. Public Health Service, report on venereal disease, 45

Venereal disease, 45-51; and the "pill," 54; commandments against, 64; causes of, 46; number of cases, 45; rate for, 50-51; see also gonorrhea, syphilis

Word of Wisdom, 35, 40, 62-63